NATURAL HISTORY

GEORGIA REVIEW BOOKS
EDITED BY Gerald Maa

NATURAL HISTORY

poems by
José Watanabe

translated by
Michelle Har Kim

with illustrations by
Eduardo Tokeshi

published in partnership with the
Smithsonian Asian Pacific American Center

The University of Georgia Press | Athens

First published in the English language
in the United States of America
by the University of Georgia Press
Athens, Georgia 30602
www.ugapress.org
Translation © 2022 by the University of Georgia Press
All rights reserved
Designed by Rebecca A. Norton
Set in 10/12.5 Warnock Pro
Printed and bound by Sheridan Books, Inc.
The paper in this book meets the guidelines for
permanence and durability of the Committee on
Production Guidelines for Book Longevity of the
Council on Library Resources.

Most University of Georgia Press titles are
available from popular e-book vendors.

Printed in the United States of America
26 25 24 23 22   P   5 4 3 2 1

Library of Congress Cataloging-in-Publication Data

Names: Watanabe, José, 1946–2007, author. |
Kim, Michelle Har, translator. | Tokeshi, Eduardo, 1960– illustrator.
Title: Natural history : poems / poems by José Watanabe ;
translated by Michelle Har Kim ; with illustrations by Eduardo Tokeshi.
Other titles: Historia natural. English
Description: Athens, Georgia : The University of Georgia Press ;
Smithsonian Asian Pacific American Center, 2022. | Series: Georgia
Review books | This book is a translation of Historia natural, published in
Lima, Peru, by PEISA in 1994. | Includes bibliographical references.
Identifiers: LCCN 2021054877 | ISBN 9780820362168 (paperback ; alk. paper) |
ISBN 9780820362175 (ebook)
Subjects: LCSH: Watanabe, José, 1946–2007—Translations into English. |
LCGFT: Poetry.
Classification: LCC PQ8498.33.A83 H5713 2022 | DDC 861'.64—dc23
LC record available at https://lccn.loc.gov/2021054877

Published by Pre-Textos Valencia Spain
Copyright © 2008 Estate of José Watanabe
All rights reserved

This book is a translation of *Historia natural*,
first published in Lima, Peru, by PEISA in 1994.

A mi hermana Dora,
desde hace tiempo.

To my sister Dora,
for a while now.

CONTENTS

Historia natural | Natural History

Museo interior | Inner Museum

Coda

A NORTHERN BESTIARY

Natural History by José Watanabe (1946–2007)

Life is as physical as it is fragile, said José Watanabe Varas. I believe he was referring to life's tactile, graspable quality, of living and breathing, or of slowly opening and closing one's hand. Life's thingness came into sharper relief for the Peruvian poet during his visit to Germany in 1986, the year that he turned forty. Already a noted television producer, by the mid-eighties Watanabe was also enjoying a reputation as a screenwriter and art director for Peruvian feature films. He had been to Munich once for a children's TV conference, but this later trip to Germany was of a different urgency. With special thanks to the love and counsel of German friends, Watanabe was admitted to a hospital in Hannover, where he had a small carcinoma removed from his lung. While he recovered in his foreign room, he could keenly sense his living body, that life was physical. Like a snug and conforming flesh, the feel of here and now was wondrous for the poet. Critics have described a gentle restraint, an insularity about Watanabe's literary and public persona. And yet he is remembered for having openly shared his inner trials and tribulations with many others. "I learned to love life," he told Rebecca Riger Tsurumi in 2005. He was referring both to his early German convalescence and to "The Ice Guardian" from *Cosas del cuerpo* (Bodily Things, 1999):

> You cannot love what so quickly fades.
> Love swiftly, said the sun.
> And so I learned, in his perverse and fiery kingdom,
> to fulfill life:
> I am the guardian of ice.

Threads of ephemerality shimmer throughout Watanabe's oeuvre and mesh themselves into the wattle and daub of *Natural History*. In "The Cure," a child is healed by his mother, at home. Versed in natural remedies and local knowledges of sickness and healing, as many mothers are, the narrator's mother holds up an egg in her hand and brushes it across her son's body. In this ritual cleansing, a limpia con huevo, an illness can be funneled away from a human body and into the simpler form of a fresh chicken egg.

> Life is physical.
> And with that conviction she rubbed the egg against my
> > body
> and so she would prevail.

Bodily sense, or what is viscerally understandable in Watanabe, is not a concept intended to prod the classical split between human body and mind. It is rather an observation about how we, stodgy with anthropocentricity and our own extraordinariness, stand to gain from a heightened awareness of the multitudinous livings among us. The royal human "we," ostensible movers and shakers of qualified global life, is demoted here. It is a curious demotion that gives a clarity to what anthropologist Marisol de la Cadena has described as "the relational condition between humans and other-than-human beings." Bodily sense, in other words, is a face-to-faceness with our Others—those with whom we have always shared the planet, however inert, dead, or robustly alive.

Camilo Fernández Cozman likens Watanabe's *Historia natural* to the medieval bestiary, the popular European compendium of real and fantastic animals. The illuminated mini-encyclopedias featured images of tigers, porcupines, and griffins, for instance, along with writings about animal oddities and Aesop-like stories of moral instruction. Bestiaries also served as virtual playgrounds for the imagination, at times mirroring anxieties about the kinds of life alleged to exist beyond Europe's flat horizons. Closer to the early modern era, bestiaries grappled with emerging colonialities that gave way to a newly global world. Latin American authors like Juan José Arreola, Kátia Bandeira de Mello Gerlach, and Nicolás Guillén, among others, are part of the pantheon of writers who explore the bestiary as a literary form, say, from Pliny the Elder to K-Ming Chang. Like Watanabe, they fashion their bestiaries with respect to their peculiar lifeworlds and languages.

A catalog of Aristotelian observation and fascination, *Natural History* invokes the field of inquiry that shares its name. Ecologist Thomas L. Fleischner describes the body of knowledge called natural history as "a practice of intentional, focused attentiveness and receptivity to the more-than-human world." It's as if the book hands us a pair of insect antennae, to put a stop to our overwordy cogitations and to let us just feel around. Both living and abiotic enjoy equal footing here, whether a pale pair of ears, the wafting scent of parsley, or a mound of potatoes whose thirsty, human faces look so much like our own. As an atlas of sorts, *Natural History* tours us across bone-dry deserts and cliffs, seasonal rushes of water, and jagged ocean beaches. It is tempting to take these landscapes as emblematic of Peru's astounding geography as a whole. Unassuming citation of places like Huanchaco, Cajamarca, and the Moche Valley, however, re-orient us toward the Peruvian north. Among the country's northern subdivisions is La Libertad, the sole region to boast all aspects of Peru's geographical triumvirate: the Amazon, the Andes, and the Pacific coast. Halfway up La Libertad's shores, about a hundred miles north of Lima, is the small city of Laredo, Watanabe's cherished hometown and childhood realm.

In the day of the growing and bustling Watanabe family, Laredo was a rural sugar-plantation town. Its idyllic spaces reverberate through many of the maestro's poems. "My pueblo was a tranquil, peaceful pueblo," he once told journalist Maribel De Paz, "with people that would say hi from a distance." One fine day, José's father Harumi decided to have a go at the Lotería de Lima y Callao—and found himself holding a winning lottery ticket. Its lucky earnings enabled the entire Watanabe clan to relocate to the city of Trujillo, the capital of the La Libertad region. For José's parents, the move away from Laredo's small-town environs would be a return to the city where Harumi, an issei migrant who arrived in Callao in 1919, first met José's mother Paula—"a mestiza Peruvian," our poet makes clear. In Trujillo, José now had access to secondary schooling. He found himself enrolled, wide-eyed, at the very institution once attended by a teenage César Vallejo.

Watanabe fans are scattered, I believe, across Spanish- and Portuguese-speaking Latin America and Europe, Scotland, Germany, France, Italy, and Japan. A Polish translator once found me at a conference to tell me how much she loved the maestro's poetry. The posthumous *Poesía completa* (The Complete Poems, 2008) unites Watanabe's seven original volumes of verse, including *La piedra alada* (The Winged Stone, 2005) and *Habitó entre nosotros* (He Lived Among Us, 2002). The omega *Banderas detrás de la niebla* (Flags Behind the Fog) was released in 2006, the year before his death at the age of sixty-one. The poet's free-verse, one-act, and one-woman rendition of Sophocles' *Antígona* was debuted in 2000 by the renowned el Grupo Cultural Yuyachkani. A monument to Peru's desaparecidos, the play continues to honor the tens of thousands who disappeared amid the nation's recent decades of terror and armed conflict. With his colleagues Amelia Morimoto and Oscar Chambi, Watanabe is coauthor of *La memoria del ojo: Cien años de presencia japonesa en el Perú* (Memory of the Eye: One Hundred Years of Japanese Presence in Peru, 1999), a large-format collection of photographs and writings that narrate moments of an ordinary and thriving migrant community and of the abrupt confusion and loss that followed the northward deportations of more than eighteen hundred Japanese Peruvians to U.S. detention camps during World War II.

Albúm de familia (Family Album), Watanabe's first collection of poetry, published in 1971, enjoyed a reception that introduced the twentysomething to Peru as one of its brightest new bards. Like the narrator of "Song of the Sunday Fisherman," Watanabe had eked out a zone of security amid a vast, oceanic machine. A canonized yet anomalous member of his literary time, he chose not to publish during the era emblematized by the great umbrella of Peruvian authors dubbed The Generation of the Seventies, and by the fractious and anti-establishment literary clusters known as Estación Reunida and Hora Zero. "Pepe," aka "Wata," or "el chino" (the latter with "no insulting or offensive connotation," he assures those of us clutching our pearls), took a step back from the reigning ethos of his contemporaries. It was impossible to speak for all artists with a single conceptual frame, he later explained. In interviews where the maestro avidly recalls the rifting horizons from which his own work also emerged, one can still feel the warmth of his unpretentiousness, of his fabulous gruff voice, and of the torch he always held for a poetics of ordinary revelation. An enchanting shrug could always fence off the technical allure of the past, like that of *Albúm*'s "Tragic Poem with Uncertain Comic Success":

> My family has no doctor
> > no priest or housecalls
> and we spread out on the beach
> hearty beneath the summer sun
>
> [. . . . .]
> For years no one's contemplated our lives on the shore
> but us
> lounging and brown under the summer sun
> like waiting for the hiss of a switch
> > at our bellies
> > at our heads
> > > nothing remarkable
> > > nothing remarkable.

Watanabe's second collection of poems, *El huso de la palabra* (The Spindle of the Word), stocked Peruvian bookshelves in 1989. It was eighteen years after *Albúm*, and much ado had been made about its prolonged demand for patience. The book's chorus of accolades was joined by various critics who proclaimed it to be the most important poetic work of its Peruvian decade. Marcos Katz Montiel has observed how Watanabe's spindle, *el huso*, and its homonym *el uso* hark of the quipu, the Incan necklace whose brailled archive was delicately knotted into its plant or animal fibers. Both words invoke the spectacular Andean textile traditions for which Peru is known. "The creation of textile-texts, from quipu to woven blankets," says Katz, "utilized spindles for yarns and threads, and thus words as well."

Published in 1994, *Historia natural* was the book Watanabe claimed to have nailed his intended thematic of life's evanescence. One may also note the blossoming of a deceptively compact and stark free-verse style. The section "Inner Museum," the book's own art alcove, pays ekphrastic homage to works by Francisco Goya, Edvard Munch, and George Segal. Watanabe's fascination with art's freedoms and vexations is often palpable; he has even described his poetry as the diary of a frustrated painter—"No pinto, yo poemo," he once mused. His sole illustrated volume of original verse, *Natural History* is the poet's collaboration with his dear friend, Peruvian painter and installation artist Eduardo Tokeshi. Once the painterly brothers had outlined their duet, they began to give it flesh through cycles of animated conversation, contemplation, and (I'm sure furious) scribbling. Each section of the book is heralded by a brusque pen-and-ink drawing by Tokeshi, creator of the solemn earth- and sea-toned collage on its splendid cover.

In haunting accord with the poems nearby, the Okinawan Peruvian artist's hybrid, Francis Bacon–like "men" look bizarrely like us—but then again, not really. They snub our assignments of metaphor and have no interest in being any one species or body. But they allow us to savor the counterpoint of Watanabe's gruff, lenient voice and Tokeshi's operatic tenor: the poet reading his ever-morphing lines aloud to his colega, as the artist intently listens, slowly waving his long, brushy antenna. The cycles continued on (very late into the evenings, I presume, with intense thought and banter), in a process resembling that of Michael Hardt and Antonio Negri, the philosopher duo known to get together to swap ideas and readings before each returns to draft his own part of a shared work, each author writing as if he were the other.

And so we are gifted with this bestiary of illusory simplicities, myths, and bodily things; a book whose unmetered verses, like many Spanish-language phrases to the Anglophone ear, will find you nodding to their vocalic flows. Like the glassy flesh of some cactus fruits, Watanabe's sheer language will draw you close and ask how different you really are from a falcon, or a stone. It can transform you into an explicit bird of passage, a floating head with no body, or some other graft of what is, and what is not, your self. Pay attention to the poems that are known to hop around and suddenly divide into multiple demands for your patience, or a more open mind. It is through the multitude, after all, that we sense and comprise the heft of another body—the common and mundane mundo, a place whose ordinary secrets are worth our undivided attention.

BIBLIOGRAPHY

Arthur, Paul Longley. "Blank Spaces for the Imagination." In *Virtual Voyages: Travel Writing and the Antipodes, 1605–1837*, by Paul Longley Arthur, 1–32. Anthem Press, 2010.

"Book of Beasts: The Bestiary in the Medieval World." *The Getty Museum*. getty.edu/art/exhibitions/bestiary/inner.html.

de la Cadena, Marisol. "Indigenous Cosmopolitics in the Andes: Conceptual Reflections beyond 'Politics.'" *CUAN Cultural Anthropology* 25, no. 2 (2010).

De Paz, Maribel. *El ombligo en el adobe: Asedios a José Watanabe*. Grupo Editorial Mesa Redonda, 2010.

Favela Bustillo, Tania. "De la lengua materna y sus historias." *Mitologías hoy* 15 (June 2017). doi:10.5565/rev/mitologias.440.

Fernández Cozman, Camilo. "*Historia natural*: El bestiario a la orilla del mito." In *Mito, cuerpo y modernidad en la poesía de José Watanabe*, by Camilo Cozman Fernández. Cuerpo de la Metáfora Editores / APSAV, 2008.

Fleischner, Thomas L. "Why Natural History Matters." *Journal of Natural History Education and Experience* 5 (2011): 21–24.

Flores Sarmiento, Ricardo. "Poesía y facetas de José Watanabe: 10 años sin el vate." *Casa de la Literatura Peruana*, April 2017. casadelaliteratura.gob.pe/poesia-facetas-jose-watanabe-10 -anos-sin-vate/.

Hardt, Michael. "How to Write with Four Hands." *Genre* 46, no. 2 (July 2013): 175–82. doi:10.1215/00166928-2088007.

Harney, Stefano, and Fred Moten. "Conversación Los Abajocomunes." Interview by Yollotl Gómez Alvarado, Juan Pablo Anaya, Luciano Concheiro, Cristina Rivera Garza, and Aline Hernández. *New Inquiry*, September 5, 2018. thenewinquiry.com/conversacion-los-abajocomunes/.

Montiel, Marco Katz. "José Watanabe y la palabra del huso." *Kaikan*, June 2013.

Shulz-Cruz, Bernard. "Cuatro bestiarios, cuatro visiones: Borges, Arreola, Neruda y Guillén." *Anales de literatura hispanoamericana*, no. 21 (1992).

Watanabe, José. *Albúm de familia*. Ausonia, 1971.

———. *Antígona: Versión libre de la tragedia de Sófocles*. Yuyachkani

/ Comisión de derechos humanos, 2000.

———. *Banderas detras de la niebla*. PEISA, 2006.

———. *Cosas del cuerpo*. Caballo Rojo, 1999.

———. " 'El estilo es el lugar donde poso mi alma': Una entrevista con José Watanabe." Interview by Alonso Rabí do Carmo. *Quehacer* 124 (2000).

———. *El huso de la palabra*. Seglusa Editores / Editorial Colmillo Blanco, 1989.

———. "Interview Five: Entrevista con José Watanabe Varas (Laredo, 1946–2007) el 30 de junio 2005 en Lima, Perú y un correo electrónico de 2005." In *The Closed Hand: Images of the Japanese in Modern Peruvian Literature*, by Rebecca Riger Tsurumi, 231–44. Purdue University Press, 2012.

———. *Habitó entre nosotros*. Pontificia Universidad Católica del Perú Fondo Editorial, 2002.

———. *Historia natural*. PEISA, 1994.

———. *La piedra alada*. PEISA, 2005.

———. " 'Los poetas dejamos de ser profetas hace tiempo': Entrevista a José Watanabe." Interview by Arturo Delgado Galimberti. *Buzon Dazibao: Antes y después del salto al vacío* blog, January 30, 2012. buzondazibao.blogspot.com/2012/01/los-poetas -dejamos-de-ser-profetas-hace.html.

———. *Path Through the Canefields*. Translated by C. A. De Lomellini and David Tipton. White Adder Press, 1997.

———. *Poesía completa*. Pre-Textos, 2008.

Watanabe, José, Amelia Morimoto, and Oscar Chambi. *La memoria del ojo: Cien años de presencia japonesa en el Perú*. Fondo Editorial del Congreso del Perú, 1999.

NATURAL HISTORY

LA ZARZA | THE BRAMBLE

Regreso a mi pueblo:
Todo lo que encuentro y toco
se vuelve zarza.

I come home:
All I come across and touch
turns to bramble.

—Kobayashi Issa

La estación del arenal

La prodigiosa lagartija corre
                    y ya no la veo más.
Oculta entre el color del médano, imperturbable, me observa
mientras el halcón huye de la resolana
y la arena cae suavemente desde las trombas de aire
sobre nadie.
Ningún ruido la inquieta. Huiría
si resonara en el aire lo que confusamente está dentro de mí:
discrimino una campana, la estridencia
de un tren
y un balido de oveja sobre las espaldas de un viajero.
Esta era la estación del arenal.
Queda un trecho de la vía desdibujada por la herrumbre,
un durmiente se quiebra como una hojarasca,
y ninguna sombra: el desierto calcinó los ficus
y sembró
sus propias plantas de largas espinas que se ensañan
                    en el esqueleto de una cabra.
Aquí la única sustancia viva es la arena, y nadie
que duerma en las bancas rotas del andén
                    la sacude de su sombrero.
Abandono este lugar. Y yéndome siento una porosidad en mi
                              propio cuerpo,
una herencia: aquí mi madre ofrecía su vendeja de frutas
a los viajeros. La siento correr
a mis espaldas
como un cuerpo de arena
que sin cesar se arma y se desintegra con su canasta.

The Station of the Sands

The prodigious lizard scampers
          and I no longer see it.
It hides in the hue of the dune, imperturbable, observing me
as the falcon flies off from the glare of the sun
sand falling softly from the whirls of air
upon no one.
No sound disturbs it. It would flee
were the air to ring with what bewilders me within:
I make out a ting, the stridency
of a train
and the bleat of a sheep on a passenger's shoulders.
This used to be the station of these sands.
What remains is a stretch of rail blurred by rust,
a sleeping body crackling like a heap of leaves,
and no shade in sight: the desert burnt off the ficus
and seeded
its own gangling and long-thorned plants that torment
          the skeleton of a goat.
The one live substance here is sand, and no one
who sleeps on this platform's broken benches
          shakes it from his hat.
I'm leaving this place. And as I turn I feel a porosity in my
          own body,
an inheritance: here my mother offered her wares of fruit
to travelers. I feel her rush
behind me
like a relentless body of sand
surging up and disintegrating with her basket.

En el desierto de Olmos

El viejo talador de espinos para carbón de palo
cuelga en el dintel de su cabaña
una obstinada lámpara de querosene,
y sobre la arena
se extiende un semicírculo de luz hospitalaria.

Este es nuestro pequeño espacio de confianza.

Más allá de la sutil frontera, en la oscuridad,
nos atisba la repugnante fauna que el viejo crea,
los imposibles injertos de los seres del aire y la tierra
y que hoy son para su propio y vivo miedo:
           la imaginación trabaja sola, aun en contra.

La iguana sí es verdadera, aunque mítica. El viejo la decapita
y la desangra sobre un cacharro indigno,
y el perro lame la cuajarada roja como si fuera su vicio.

Rápida es olorosa
la blanca carne de la iguana en la baqueta de asar.
El viejo la destaza y comemos
        y el perro espera paciente los delicados huesos.

Impensadamente
arrojo los huesos fuera de la luz
y tras ellos el animal entra en el país nocturno y enemigo.

Desde la oscuridad aúlla estremecido
y seguramente queriendo alcanzar
           entre la inestable arena
con ansia
nuestro pequeño espacio de confianza.
Oigo entonces el reproche del viejo: deja los huesos cerca,
el perro
también es paisano.

At the Desert of Olmos

The old woodcutter of hawthorn for charcoal
hangs on his cabin lintel
a stubborn kerosene lamp,
and across the sand
spreads a half-circle of welcoming light.

This is our little sanctuary.

Past the faint border, from the dark,
leer the repulsive fauna he creates,
impossible grafts of air- and land-borne beasts
today bred for his bright-eyed fear:
        the imagination works alone, and yet against.

The iguana is real, though mythical. The elder cuts away its head
and bleeds it over a paltry pot,
as the dog laps the red curdle like it was a vice.

Quick the smell
white iguana meat on the roasting spit.
The old man carves it and we eat
      as the dog waits patient for the delicate bones.

Heedlessly
I fling the bones outside the light
and the animal trails them into night and hostile country.

Shivering in the dark it howls
surely hoping to make it back
        across the unpredictable sand
and pining
for our little sanctuary.
Then I hear the old man's reproach: keep the bones close,
the dog
is one of us.

El acuerdo

No sé si el chacarero tuvo intención,
pero me dio su silla y me dejó mirando este admirable acuerdo:
el pájaro chotacabras
está posado sobre la espalda del toro, confiadamente, sabiendo
que de las ancas a los cuernos
al toro le recorre siempre una pulsación agresiva.
Pero con el chotacabras allí,
pareciera que la bestia entra en paz, en ocio, oye
el sonido sedante de las uñas del pájaro rascando su piel,
siente
la lengüita
que le limpia la sangre de la matadura
y el ala desplegada que le barre el polvo
y el pico como delicado instrumento de enfermera
buscándole
las larvas que le muerden bajo la piel.
El pájaro topiquero gana así su alimento.
Ese es el intercambio ordinario,
pero el chotacabras gana más: encima del lomo
regusta
una vasta ternura que nadie sospecha, la paradoja
de la bestia.

The Pact

I'm not sure if the farmer meant to,
but he gave up his seat and left me watching this remarkable pact:
a nightjar bird
perched on a bull's back, confidently, knowing
that from horns to haunches
an aggressive pulse always runs through the bull.
Though with the nightjar there,
it's like the beast enters peace, an idleness, he listens
to the soothing sound of the bird's claws that scrape his skin,
he feels
the little tongue
that cleans blood off the chafe of the harness
and the splayed wing brushing off dust
and the beak like the delicate tool of a nurse
prodding him
for the larvae that bite beneath his skin.
It's how the attendant bird earns its food.
A routine exchange,
but the nightjar gains more: on the back of the bull
it savors
a vast and unsuspected tenderness, the paradox
of the beast.

En el cauce vacío

En verano,
según ley de aguas, el río Vichanzao no viene a los cañaverales.
Los parceleros lo detienen arriba
                    y lo conducen al panllevar.
Aquí en el cauce queda fluyendo una brisa, un río
                    invisible.
Camino pisando los cantos rodados enterrados en el limo
y mirando los charcos donde sobreviven diminutos peces grises
que muerden el reflejo de mi rostro.
Los pequeños sorbedores de mocos ya no los atrapamos en botellas.
Tampoco tejemos trampas para camarones
                    y nuestro lejano bullicio se esfuma
sin dolor.
Supuse más dolor. En el regreso todo se convierte en zarza,
                    dijo Issa.
Pero yo camino extrañamente aliviado,
                    ni herido ni culposo,
por el cauce
en cuyas altas paredes asoman raíces de sauces. Las muerdo
y este sabor amargo es la única resistencia que hallo
mientras avanzo contra la corriente.

In the Dry Riverbed

In summer,
due to water law, the Vichanzao River won't come to the canefields.
The plot holders keep it above
                        and route it toward more vital fields.
Here in the riverbed lingers a breeze, a stream
                        unseen.
I walk stepping on rocks buried into the silt
and peering in puddles where tiny grey fish survive
and nibble at my face's reflection.
We snot-nosed kids no longer catch them in bottles
or weave traps for shrimp
                        and our faraway ruckus fades
without pain.
I imagined more pain. Everything turns to bramble on returning,
                        said Issa.
But I walk with odd levity,
                        neither wounded nor guilty,
up the riverbed
from whose high walls bulge roots of willows. I chew them
and their bitter flavor is the one resistance I come across
as I move against the current.

Camposanto

Por dejadez de municipio
el muro perimétrico que guardaba a los muertos
        es un largo escombro de adobes.
Era alto y detenía al viento
que ahora dispersa y confunde a su antojo
las ofrendas que dejamos sobre la tierra combada de las tumbas.

Las flores viajan de un muerto a otro, o naranjas
resecas
o bocadillos podridos en hojas de plátano.
Los deudos callamos
porque la muerte al fin está redistribuyendo todo entre todos.

Todavía no es escombro una alta y robusta columna de barro.
                        Resiste
y se yergue
coronada por una gran esfera revocada con yeso.
Las grietas y desprendimientos de revoque
        le han dibujado duras facciones casuales,
y la columna es un ángel marcial y mutilado de alas,
                        un resentido.
En las tardes, cuando la luz desciende en haces, bíblica,
                él, perverso, dice que no,
pero la luz penetra los túmulos hasta tocar la frente de los muertos
para decirles que sí,
que la promesa sí.

Cemetery

Due to municipal neglect
the perimeter wall that used to harbor the dead
    is a heap of adobe.
It stood tall and tamed the winds
that confuse and swat around
the offerings we leave on the tombs' wrangled earth.

Flowers flit from one body to another, or shriveled
oranges
or decaying sandwiches in banana leaves.
We relatives keep quiet
as death finally reshuffles all among all.

A hale and lofty clay column will not yield to detritus.
                    It resists
and rises
crowned in a magnificent plaster sphere.
Cracks and keen fissures
    have drawn it harsh features,
and the pillar is a battle angel torn from his wings,
                embittered.
In late afternoons, as fingers of light descend, biblical,
        he, perverse, says no,
but the light seeps into the tombs to touch the foreheads of the dead
to tell them yes,
the promise is yes.

EL OTRO CUERPO | THE OTHER BODY

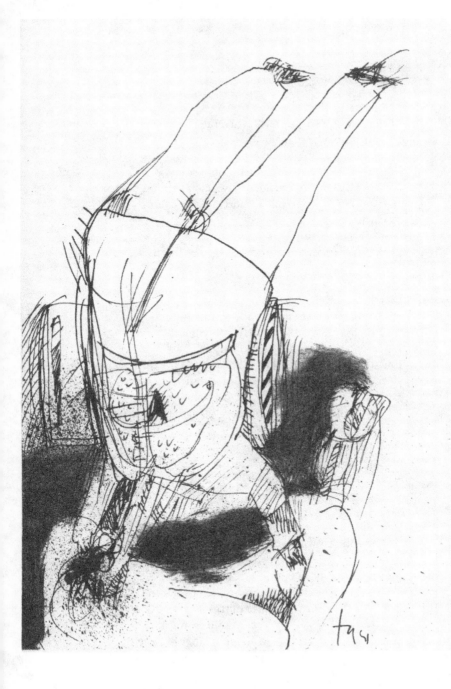

El ciervo

El ciervo es mi sueño más recurrente.
Siendo animal de manada aparece mirándome con alzada
                    y orgullo
                            de hombre solo.
A media distancia pasta en un espacio pequeño, y alrededor
                    todo petrificado, ningún cuerpo
de carne
que se le compare.
El ciervo se mueve como articulado por fuertes elásticos
                    internos
que convergen en un poderoso órgano desconocido y central.
De allí su caminar gracioso
                que disimula su enorme fuerza
                        elástica, su potencial
                            de vuelo.
Imaginemos la eventualidad de un cazador y de un certero disparo,
ya el ciervo está desarrollando su instantáneo salto
                        en el cielo.
La jauría sólo llegará a su primera sangre, a la sorprendida,
y luego ni lamerá
                ninguna
porque en el ascenso
el ciervo curará su herida
                        con simple
                        saliva.

Y aterrizado y salvo aparecerá otra noche en mi sueño
                de hipocondriaco.
Mi miedo volverá a cubrirlo de atributos
                de inmortal. Y así mirándolo
            yo mismo me miro
                        pero sólo en mi sueño
porque la voz de mi vigilia no entra allí, y el ciervo
                nunca oye
                mi cólera:
¡no eres de vuelo y morirás en el suelo, mordido
                    por los perros!

The Stag

My most frequent dream is of the stag.
As a herd animal it comes and watches me with the pride
                    and stature
                        of a lone man.
It grazes on a patch at mid-distance, and around it
                    everything is petrified, no body
of flesh
can compare.
The stag lithely moves as if jointed with thick
                        inner bands
that converge in a mighty organ unfamiliar and prime.
And so its funny gait
            belies its enormous elastic
                    force, its promise
                        of flight.
Imagine a hunter's sure shot,
the stag now unfurling an instant leap
                    into sky.
The pack closes in on its first, startled blood,
and then licks
            no other
for in its ascent
the stag heals its own wound
                    with simple
                        saliva.

Safe on the ground it will appear some other night
                        in my hypochondriac dreams.
My fear will cloak it again with features
                    of an immortal. And as I watch it
            I see myself
                    sleeping
for my vigilant voice won't go in, and the stag
            never hears
            my rage:
you're not from the air so don't die on the ground, mauled
                    by those hounds!

La oruga

Te he visto ondulando bajo las cucardas, penosamente,
                                        trabajosamente,
pero sé que mañana serás del aire.

Hace mucho supe que no eras un animal terminado
y como entonces
arrodillado y trémulo
te pregunto:
¿Sabes que mañana serás del aire?
¿Te han advertido que esas dos molestias aún invisibles
serán tus alas?
¿Te han dicho cuánto duelen al abrirse
o sólo sentirás de pronto una levedad, una turbación
y un infinito escalofrío subiéndote desde el culo?

Tú ignoras el gran prestigio que tienen los seres del aire
y tal vez mirándote las alas no te reconozcas
y quieras renunciar,
pero ya no: debes ir al aire y no con nosotros.

Mañana miraré sobre las cucardas, o más arriba.
Haz que te vea,
quiero saber si es muy doloroso el aligerarse para volar.
Hazme saber
si acaso es mejor no despejar nunca la barriga de la tierra.

The Caterpillar

I've seen you wriggle under the hibiscus, onerously,
                                        laboriously,
but I know tomorrow you'll belong to the air.

For a while I've known you were not a finished animal
kneeling and shivering
like then
I ask:
Do you know that tomorrow you'll be up in the air?
Have they warned you of that invisible pair of tender spots
that will be your wings?
Have they told you how it hurts to splay them
or that you'll just feel a sudden buoyancy, some turbulence
and a bottomless chill that lifts you off your butt?

You've no clue about the grand prestige of creatures of the air
and you may not recognize yourself in wings
and might just want to quit,
but don't: you must go to the air and not with us.

Tomorrow I'll look for you on the hibiscus, or higher.
Let me see,
to know how painful it can be to lighten up and fly.
Let me know
if it might be best to never clear this belly off the earth.

Las rodillas

Los potrillos abrevan. Sorben agua y enseguida alzan el cuello
                    y respiran la luz.
En este sereno ramal del río Moche la luz es respirable.
Los caballos
ya saciados
van a frotarse los flancos contra la corteza de los pinos,
placer que les sacude graciosamente las jetas.
Arriba hay dura grava,
pero los caballos y yo descansamos en la yerba que se tiende
y crea la pequeña pradera
por donde transcurre el agua y donde la luz
                    danza.
Este ramal fue abierto por los chimús,
pero en el siglo XVII fue sepultado por una rodante pedrea
                    de terremoto.
Los huanchaqueros dicen que su Deán, Don Antonio de Saavedra,
al ver los sembríos muertos,
se arrodilló delante del agua represada
y así avanzó, rompiendo las piedras con sus rodillas, y el agua
como perro
lo seguía.
Y yo miro mis rodillas, la unión de mis huesos
                    más duros, y la luz
las abrillanta, les miente poder, las decanta
riscosas
                    como el vestigio
del cuerpo consistente que nunca tuve, ese cuerpo
no quebradizo
                    que sueño para mi vulnerable blandura.
Nunca fui de materia más consistente. Y el sueño
                    es tan compasivo como inútil.

En una urna de la iglesia de Huanchaco
está el esqueleto del Deán de Saavedra. Estoy seguro
que sus sagradas rodillas
también se dispersarían como polvo en esta luz.

Knees

The colts drink. They sip water and raise their necks
                    to breathe the light.
In this serene branch of the Moche River the light is breathable.
The horses
now sated
are going to scrub their flanks against the piney bark,
a funny pleasure that rumbles their snouts.
Up above the gravel is hard,
but the horses and I unwind in this grass that spreads
into a small meadow
where water runs and the light
                    dances.
This branch was opened by the Chimú,
but in the seventeenth century was buried in an earthquake's
                    roiling hail.
The Huanchaqueros say their commander, Don Antonio de Saavedra,
seeing the deadened fields,
knelt to the dammed-up water
and advanced, crushing rocks with his knees, as the water
like a dog
trailed behind.
And I see my knees, the crux of my toughest
                    bones, as the light
burnishes them, feigns their power, decants their
crags
                    like a vestige
of the solid body I never had, the body
unbreakable
                    that I dream for my vulnerable frailty.
I was never made of any matter more consistent. And the dream
                    is as compassionate as it is useless.

In an urn at the Church of Huanchaco
is the skeleton of Dean de Saavedra. I am sure
his sacred knees
would scatter too like dust in this light.

El gato

Estoy esperando la vuelta del gato desconocido
    que cruzó el alféizar de mi ventana.
El alféizar corre a lo largo de varias ventanas. No tiene
otro camino. Volverá
y esta vez mi imagen le será más cordial.

Pasó arrogante como un bello inmortal. Los gatos ignoran
la contingencia de los torpes,
                tropezar y caer.
Miden tan bien sus pasos cuando cazan o fugan, y nunca
nunca cara de extraviados. Así nos infunden en la mente
su propio mito.
Y los mininos de viejas no los contradicen
porque gato es gato, dignísima fiera cuando la vieja duerme.

Los gatos son peligrosos para la poesía, pronto
acumulan adjetivos, mucho provocan, mucho seducen.
Por eso no espero limpiamente la vuelta del gato,
la mucha belleza me hace siempre perverso. Y digo:
está caído en la vereda, inmóvil, dirigiendo
hacia mi altísima ventana
        su última y fosforescente mirada.

The Cat

I await the return of the roving cat
        that walked across my windowsill.
The sill runs the length of several windows. There is
no other route. It will come back
and next time I'll be more cordial.

It strutted arrogantly by like a beautful immortal. Cats know nothing
about slips and falls,
          or torpid hesitations.
They calibrate their steps when they hunt or dart away, and never
without preoccupation. That's how they instill their myth
within our minds.
And old ladies' kitties won't disagree
for a cat is a cat, such a dignified beast when an old lady sleeps.

Cats are dangerous for poetry, too promptly
accruing adjectives, provoking here, seducing there.
So I'm not really waiting for the cat to return,
all that beauty just depraves me. I say:
it's sprawled upon the sidewalk, motionless, directing
at my lofty window
        its final and phosphorescent stare.

El puente

Las columnas herrumbradas por el aire delgado
de la altura
suben desde las pendientes de la quebrada y sostienen con gruesos
                                                   remaches
los travesaños de hierro.
Hay miles de remaches en la estructura del puente
pero en el centro hay un solo fijando el encuentro
de todas las fuerzas, uno solo, insospechado y firme,
             evitando que el mundo se venga abajo.
Aquí alguna vez un hombre se sentó a horcajadas, hercúleo,
                   sobre el abismo
y selló el remache decisivo, acero al rojo y con esquirlas.
Imagina la acción tensa y peligrosa de su brazo
golpeando acompasado
como si nos transmitiera serenamente un mensaje:
                  nadie asegura el mundo en su contra.
El remache
permite el paso del tren de los metales y del tren de los migrantes
y el paso contrario de los que vamos a mirar sus paisajes y
                                   cortamontes.
Y mientras cruzas el puente y miras aterrado el vacío de desfiladero
siente el interminable poder de ese hombre,
pero imagínalo después caminando como cualquiera,
                  sin alardes,
hacia los viejos campamentos desmontados
         donde durmió sobre un pellejo su sincero cansancio.

The Bridge

The columns rusted by the altitude's
thin air
rise from the ravine's slopes and with thick rivets suspend
crossbeams of iron.
Thousands of rivets are in the frame of the bridge
but only one in the center to fix the encounter
of forces, just one, unsuspecting and firm,
      stopping the world from plunging below.
A man straddled here, Herculean,
         above the abyss
and sealed the decisive rivet, steel-red and splintering.
Imagine the treacherous tension of his arm's
measured pounding
as if unhurriedly transmitting a message:
      no one secures the world against itself.
The rivet
allows the passage of metal freight and migrant trains
and those of us seeing the country and spring festivals in the other
         direction.
And when you cross the bridge and peer into the gorge's terrible void
feel the man's boundless power,
then imagine him walking like anyone else,
      without fanfare,
back to the stripped-down old encampments
    where on a hide he slept off his sincere exhaustion.

HISTORIA NATURAL | NATURAL HISTORY

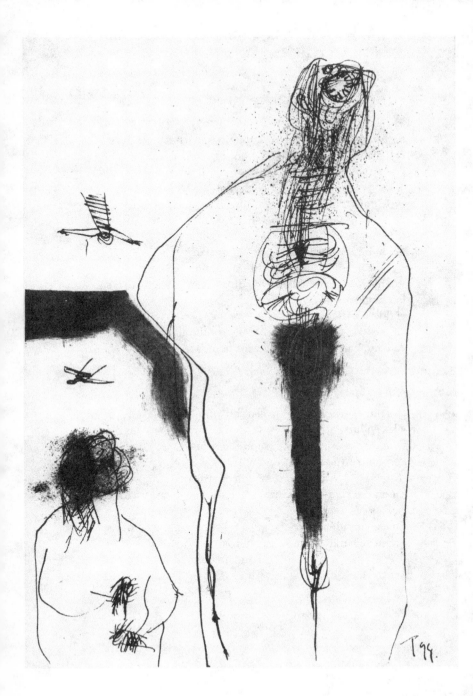

La cura

El cascarón liso del huevo
sostenido en el cuenco de la mano materna
resbalada por el cuerpo del hijo, allá en el norte.
Eso vi:
          una mujer más elemental que tú
espantando a la muerte con ritos caseros, cantando
             con un huevo en la mano, sacerdotisa
más modesta no he visto.
Yo la miraba desgranar sobre su regazo
            los maíces de la comida
mientras el perro callejero se disolvía en el relente del sol
lamiendo
el dolor arrojado a la tierra
             junto con el huevo del milagro.
Así era. La vida pasaba sin aspavientos
             entre gente parca, padre y madre
que me preguntaban por mi alivio. El único valor
era vivir.
Las nubes pasaban por la claraboya
y las gallinas alineaban en su vientre sus santas ovas
y mi madre esperaba nuevamente el más fresco huevo
con un convencimiento:
             la vida es física.
Y con ese convencimiento frotaba el huevo contra mi cuerpo
y así podía vencer.
En ese mundo quieto y seguro fui curado para siempre.
En mí se harán todos los milagros. Eso vi,
          qué no habré visto.

The Cure

The smooth shell of an egg
held up in the palm of the maternal hand
brushes over the body of a son, out there in the north.
That's what I saw:
      a woman more elemental than you
startling death with folk rites, chanting
        egg in hand, a priestess
more modest I have not seen.
On her lap I watched her shell
        the evening meal's corn
as the stray dog dissolved in the dew of late sun
lapping
the pain hurled at the ground
        alongside the miraculous egg.
That's how it was. Life went on without much fuss
        among frugal people, father and mother
who asked how I felt. The sole value
was to live.
Clouds passed across the open skylight
as hens aligned their holy ova inside their wombs
and my mother waited once more for the freshest egg
with a certainty:
        life is physical.
And with that conviction she rubbed the egg against my body
and so she would prevail.
In that still and certain world I was cured forever.
In me all miracles shall be done. That's what I saw,
        and what haven't I seen.

El esqueleto

Un hueso y otro hueso, los innumerables,
están unidos por el delgado alambre que atraviesa
el canal donde estuvo el tuétano.
Y así cuelga
y yo sólo puedo confirmar que cuelga solamente.
No puedo atribuirle desgano, indiferencia o desdén.
Él ya está libre de esos ánimos nuestros. La carne
              ya los ha pagado.
Mi amigo lo compró para su didáctica de médico
y es irrespetuoso con él
              por miedo.
Yo lo zarandeo amistosamente
                    al pasar
y mi gesto tampoco lo ofende, sólo se balancea,
                    y debiera oírse una alegría,
como la dulce y múltiple algazara
del móvil o quitasueño del niño de mi amigo.
              Mas nada suena
                    y de súbito
              se propicia otro niño:
dormita enfermo en una cueva abierta hacia la noche
y no oye la algazara
sino el ruido insoportable de sonajas óseas
                    y la advertencia
del curandero que grita borracho y aterrado:
¡despierta y pelea, muchachito, la puta
de los huesos
ya viene!

The Skeleton

One bone and another bone, innumerable,
are joined by a thin wire that runs through the groove
where the marrow used to be.
And so it hangs
and I can only confirm that it hangs.
I can't ascribe it apathy, indifference or scorn.
It's free from those humors of ours. The flesh
                    has paid its dues.
My friend got it for a medical seminar
and is disrespectful with it
                out of fear.
I give it a good jostle
                    when I go by
and the gesture won't offend it either, it just sways,
                    and some revelry should sound,
like the sweet myriad jubilation
of the dreamcatcher mobile my friend got his son.
                But nothing sounds
                    and from the blue
            enjoins another child:
dozing sickly in a cave wide open toward the night
it hears not jubilation
but an unbearable jangle of bony rattles
                    and the admonition
of the drunk and unmanned curandero shouting:
Up and fight, little man, the puta
of the bones
here she comes!

La bicicleta

El monociclo es del chimpancé para sus gracias de circo
y el monstruoso tándem de los matrimonios bien coordinados.
Yo sólo quería una bicicleta de paseo, lenta, meditativa.
No una bicicleta de competencia:
        mi modo es más pausado, es necesario tiempo
para las cortesías de paso.
Nunca tuve esa bicicleta, pero me apena ahora
verla desmembrada en este sucio taller.
El viejo reparador me observa tocar lentamente cada pieza:
bellas ruedas
radioladas
que bien existen solas aunque no sirvan para nada,
el cuerpo central perfecto como un ideograma,
el timón como astas de un animal que se ha expuesto mucho
        al viento en contra
y la montura como amable palma que levanta
y aún sus negras cámaras
colgando viscerales, el rasgo repulsivo
de su belleza.
Nunca tuve esa bicicleta y eso explica
que hasta hoy no haya elaborado una filosofía
más allá de los nerviosos animales que he cabalgado,
        y siempre serán el burro, el perro y el chivo.

The Bicycle

The unicycle is for chimp circus tricks
and the hideous tandem of choreographed marriages.
I just wanted a bicycle to cruise with, meditative, slow.
Not a bike for racing:
　　　　　my style's a bit more leisurely, one needs time
for the pleasantries of cruising.
I've never had that bike, although it saddens me
to see one dismembered in this grimy shop.
The old repairman watches as I carefully touch each part:
exquisite tires
radial
each exists nicely on its own even with no purpose,
the frame flawless like an ideogram,
with handlebars like antlers long exposed
　　　　　　　　to opposing winds
and the seat a friendly palm that lifts
and even its dark inner tubes
hang visceral, the repulsive aspect
of its beauty.
I've never had this bike and that explains
why I haven't come up with a philosophy until today
apart from the jittery animals I've ridden,
　　　　and they'll always be the donkey, the dog, and the goat.

La silla perezosa

Tú que corres haciendo tanto ruido inútil
siéntate en esta perezosa vacía y descansa.
Después llamarás a esta calle la calle de las perezosas.
Hoy no es el último día del mundo, el tiempo
no ha paseado huyendo como un conejo
y los anuncios
son anuncios de nada.
Deja que se pudra en el atrio de la iglesia el carnero bicéfalo
y que las madres cobijen hijos muertos
           como huevos inútiles.
La bestia del milenio aún no ha nacido
          y la fatalidad no es inminente.
Tú, asustado muchacho, ven y reposa
       y sigue el tiempo del carpintero:
toca una perezosa, allí está tu tiempo.

Y mis manos aprecian la madera trabajada con lentitud y
                            conciencia
y sienten otras manos teñidas de resina de cedro
que impulsaron
con justo ritmo
el cepillo
sobre los listones cuya rectitud geométrica y ética
        estaba en el ojo entrecerrado del maestro.

Se acabó la calle de las perezosas
       y se acabaron los viejos de lengua gótica.
Pero la imaginación del regreso aún es posible
          sentado
en la perezosa que vino conmigo en el camión de mudanzas.
Me espera en el patio, siempre bien armada y encolada,
         durando
y provocando un deseo contra la historia, la vuelta
a los románticos talleres artesanales, todo hecho a mano
y pacientemente. Entre la viruta
un conejo
todavía dormirá el tiempo de los muchachos asustados.

Lounge Boulevard

You running around making all that racket
sit down in this empty lounge chair and relax.
You'll soon call this whole street Lounge Boulevard.
Today isn't the end of the world, time
hasn't bounded off like a rabbit
and the advertisements
are advertising nothing.
Let the two-headed ram decay in the church atrium
and let the mothers hover over their dead children
        like futile eggs.
The millennial beast hasn't even been born
          and there's no pestilence imminent.
You, frightened young man, come rest
        and take the time of the carpenter:
touch a lawn chair, there's your time.

And my hands perceive this wood wrought in conscience and
                              deliberation
and feel other hands stained with the resin of cedars
hands that drove
the plane
of timely rhythm
across the slats whose geometric and ethical rectitude
        lived in the squint of the maestro's eye.

Lounge Boulevard is no longer
        and gone are the elders who spoke Gothic.
Though imagining their return is still possible
            seated
in the lawn chair that came here with me on the moving truck.
It waits for me in the yard, ever sturdy and well-assembled,
           enduring
and inciting desire against history, a return
to the Romantic artisan atelier, everything made by hand
and patiently. Among the shavings
a rabbit
still sleeps to the time of frightened young men.

A la noche

Tiendo a la noche.

La noche profunda es silenciosa y robusta
        como una madre de faldón amplio.

Los que conocieron a doña Paula sabrán que la metáfora es
                inmejorable.

Un psicoanalista me ha explicado en su jerga
que tiendo a la noche porque facilita la vuelta
        de mi yo primario.
Y ese yo es el niño imaginario ovillado
        y en formol
que a veces despierta y me ordena que me acurruque en la cama vacía
y me obliga al goce de ese vergonzoso encogimiento.

Yo siempre supongo un lector duro y severo, desconfiado
de las muchas astucias
        de los pobrecitos poetas.
Por él me levanto y me rehago hasta tocar el cielo oscuro
y la noche empieza a transcurrir como solar.
Pero el benigno mal de la vigilia hace áspero mi rostro
        y lo desencaja levemente.
Entonces digo que agua helada me vendría bien.
Voy a la cocina.
En la canastilla de mimbre hay papas amontonadas:
        tienen lejanos relieves faciales
y están velando en la penumbra
        con sus ojillos hundidos
           y sucios de tierra.

Míralas conmigo, incompasivo lector:
cualquier papa soy yo, el primario,
        acaso nonato, y quién sabe si ya picado.

To Night

I tend to the night.

The thick night is robust and noiseless
          like a mother in a roomy skirt.

Those who knew Doña Paula will love the unbeatable metaphor.

A psychoanalyst once told me in his words
that I tend toward the night because it facilitates the return
          of my primary self.
And that imaginary self is a child wound up
          and in formaldehyde
who wakes sometimes and orders me to curl up in the empty bed
and forces me to schnuzzle back into that cringy coil.

I always suppose a harsh and exacting reader, wary
of the antics
          of poor little poets.
For you I rise and start anew by stretching into the dark sky
as night begins to pass like day.
But the mild evil of insomnia roughens my face
          and warps it a bit.
Cold water will do me some good.
I head to the kitchen.
In the wicker basket is a mound of potatoes:
          their faraway facial contours
are veiled in semidarkness
          with sunken little eyes
               and dirty bits of earth.

Watch them with me, merciless reader:
any potato am I, the primary,
          not even born, or who knows if already chopped
               away.

A los '70s

Miro las gotas que la humedad condensa lentamente
en el vidrio de mi ventana.
Detrás de las gotas pasa un muchacho con un James Dean
        en la camiseta.
James Dean, el mismo, el que nos decía
live soon, death soon
(apenas sabíamos inglés pero lo entendíamos demasiado bien).

Mi ciudad era rápida, cada día más rápida,
tenía veredas como fajas contínuas,
        pero nosotros éramos más veloces.
Qué iba a estar quieto mirando gotas en el vidrio de una ventana,
qué iba a estar tan cómodamente
de este lado
donde el calor de mi habitación me permite actos ociosos,
        el índice
        adelantándose
al camino de una y otra gota que se funden y resbalan.
Prevenir el camino parece posible, veo, casi toco
las gotas,
pero el dedo nunca acierta: el agua está del otro lado.

To the '70s

I watch beads of moisture slowly condense
on my windowpane.
Behind the droplets a kid goes by with James Dean
                on his shirt.
James Dean, the one and only, he who told us
live soon, death soon
(we hardly knew any English but we sure understood).

My city was fast, faster each day,
with sidewalks like serpentine belts,
                but we were faster.
Who wants to sit and watch drops on a glass,
why would anyone just lounge around
on this side
where the heat of my room leaves me idling,
                my finger
                gains speed
down the road where one drop and another slide and meld.
I'll avoid this route, I can see, almost touching
the droplets,
but my finger can't confirm: the water is on the other side.

Canción del pescador dominical

Dejo el anzuelo en el mar, 100 metros abajo,
y en la punta del acantilado
                una piedra recalentada
calienta mis flacas piernas y mi día permitido de sosiego.
Aquí espero mi parte de tajada, mi pez flaco y desbocado.
Y esta habilidad no es fácil
más todavía en este pequeño terreno, en la punta de despeñadero.
El mar nunca será una orquesta coherente, abajo
rompe las piedras y el espinazo de los peces lentos, y la sal
muerde el agua dulce de los ríos,
y la ventana
y el candado
son trabados por la sal, más dura en el invierno.
Sin embargo, hoy es verano
y domingo
y las damas en la playa reciben el sol de su belleza
y algunos gimnastas practican el retozo de corpore sano.
En verdad, es un día muy bello.
Aquí no es imaginable la gran serpiente de los dibujos medievales.
La única crueldad que el mar me permite es ensartar pequeños peces
desde la punta del acantilado, sitio difícil,
donde construyo a duras penas mi zona de seguridad
y espero como en ascuas mi tajada, mi sueldo.

Song of the Sunday Fisherman

I leave the hook inside the sea, 100 meters down,
and on the clifftop
        a heated rock
warms these skinny legs and my given day of rest.
Here I await my share, my scrawny gaping fish.
And the task isn't so easy
from this small terrain, up here on the bluff.
The sea will never be a coherent orchestra, down below
it breaks on rocks and spines of languid fish, as salt
stirs into the river's sweetwater,
and the window
and lock
are crusted thick with salt, even thicker in winter.
However, today is summer
and a Sunday
and the ladies on the beach are taking in their rays of beauty
and some gymnasts practice romping in their sound and hearty bodies.
Truly, what a gorgeous day.
The great serpent of medieval drawings is unimaginable here.
The one cruelty that the sea allows me is to snare little fish
from this cliff, a hard place,
where I eke out a zone of security
at the edge of my seat watching my livelihood, my lot.

La deshabitada

Interminable
pleito entre herederos mantenía la casona deshabitada y en
escombros.
Yo pasaba el ocioso día en un altillo vecino
y de ventana siempre abierta a la casona.
Cuando escribía, la contemplaba sin propósito
o buscando palabras para el poema.
En su imperceptible destrucción,
puertas y ventanas
perdían lentamente la escuadra, y pilares y vigas
dibujaban cruces que el salitre del mar cercano ennegrecía.
Una hiedra entraba en las habitaciones
como mirando
y se tejía con abuso en la quincha desconchada.
Las alimañas, confiando en la desolación, dejaron de pigmentarse
y a mi ventana trepaban cucarachas blancas
que yo mataba con terror.
El suelo se ablandaba y el gran dibujo geométrico
en las baldosas de patio
se fruncía, quería ser espiral, esperaba
el gran remolino que llevaría todo hacia el centro de la tierra.
El gran remolino vendría, sin duda, y violento.
Ante el lentísimo hundimiento de la casona,
mi altillo lucía más elevado y consistente.
Yo estaba a salvo, pero mis ojos
que siempre saben más
descubrieron
que yo miraba la casona con afinidad callada
o con aquello que las imperturbables matemáticas llaman
el común denominador.

Uninhabited

Interminable
feuds among heirs kept the mansion empty and in
shambles.
I'd saunter the day in a neighboring attic
with a window that gaped at the mansion.
When I wrote, I'd stare at it aimlessly
or when drumming up words for a poem.
In its imperceptible decline,
doors and windows
slowly lost perpendicularity, as joists and columns
formed crosses blackened by the ocean's salty residue.
A vine of ivy came into the rooms
as if looking around
and then meshed itself hard with the wattle and mud.
Vermin, trusting in the plight, stopped their pigmentations
and into my window clambered white roaches
which I killed off in fright.
The floors began to soften and the vast geometric design
on the patio tiles
puckered, wanting to spiral, and waited
for the great whirlwind to pull everything toward the earth's center.
The great whirlwind would come, no doubt, and violently.
Facing the mansion's lagging collapse,
my attic seemed higher and sound.
I was safe, but my eyes
which always know better
discovered me
watching the mansion with silent affinity
or the imperturbable mathematicians call
the common denominator.

A tus orejas

Tus orejas eran mi único y suficiente auditorio
cuando estaban a ambos lados de tu atentísima cabeza.
Pero anoche no vi tu cabeza, sólo tus orejas
como dos mariposas, dos caracoles, dos ranitas estrujadas.
No debería usar símiles para hablar de tus orejas
porque vinieron a mi sueño solamente orejas como tales,
                        desnudas,
                                como propiamente.
Mas el inconforme lenguaje prefiere nombrarlas
con figuras, con efímeros
prodigios.
Pero estos pequeños prodigios nunca cautivaron tus blancas orejas
sino los que reverencia la antropología, el folklore
                        y seguramente el miedo,
historias de asombra, mitos del pendejo pueblo mío.
Cuéntame, decías,
y a tu pedido la memoria popular era para el introito.
Y si más prodigiosa la historia, de más lejos era yo.
Amabas al recóndito
            aunque con el estimulante recelo de tus ojos
y de tu cuerpo que lentamente se rendía
para que—como quieren los Amarus—lo de abajo esté arriba.

To Your Ears

Your ears were my one and only auditorium
on both sides of your fabulously attentive head.
But last night I didn't see a head, just your ears
like two butterflies, two snails, two scrunchy little frogs.
I shouldn't use similes to talk about your ears
because they came to me in my dreams just like that,
                    naked,
                        as they should be.
Nonconformist language prefers to name them
with figures, in ephemeral
wonders.
But those little wonders could never captivate your white ears
only those revering anthropology, folklore
                        and certainly fear,
stories of amazement, myths of my swindling people.
Tell me, you'd say,
and at your behest the popular memory was the prologue.
The more prodigious the story, the further away I was.
You loved the recondite
            despite the disquieted thrill in your eyes
and your body that slowly surrendered
so that—like the Amarus desire—what's down below is up above.

La ardilla

Una ardilla cumplida, diaria, viene a mi balcón.
Recoge nerviosamente el pan que le dejo y huye al bosque.
Su huida es como guiada
por otra ardilla que sale de sí misma y la antecede
un segundo
siempre,
y aún detrás de ella va dejando otra, un ágil trazo
que se desvanece milagrosamente en el aire ordinario.
Así la ardilla va como un curioso juego óptico de veloces figuras
que nunca encajan.
Es como la vibración de alguien que corre detrás de una verja.

Este fue un ejercicio muy subjetivo de descripción
que escribí antes de la cirugía en un hospital de Hannover.
Quedó inconcluso
porque no supe conducir con claridad su sentido.
Tal vez quise hablar de los animales de vida vibrátil
              y también capaces de ser de quietud
como la ardilla que se recoge en el fondo de una cueva
e hiberna
fetal
casi muerta
              y el tiempo transcurre, pero no para ella.
O acaso quise hablar de resurrecciones. Yo buscaba
desesperadamente ese sentido. Sí,
porque cuando la ardilla vuelve trae todavía
la incredulidad de su despertar, y cambia,
                    y eventualmente
es una mujer, el verano, cualquier contento.

The Squirrel

A punctilious squirrel, every day, comes by my balcony.
It nervously collects the bread I've left and flees into the woods.
It's flight is as if guided
by another squirrel that jumps out of itself and that one is preceded
always
by a second,
and there's another behind that one, a nimble line
miraculously vanishing into ordinary air.
So the squirrel takes off in an optic game of zooming figures
that never fit together.
Like the vibration of someone running along the other side of a fence.

This was a subjective exercise in description
that I wrote before my surgery at a hospital in Hannover.
It was unfinished
because I didn't know how to convey its meaning clearly.
Maybe I meant to talk about vibrating animals
              also capable of stillness
like the squirrel who retreats into the thickness of its den
and hibernates
fetal
nearly dead
              as time goes on, but not for it.
Or maybe I meant to talk about resurrections. I've looked back
for them desperately. Yes,
because when the squirrel returns it still brings
the incredulity of its awakening, and it changes,
              and eventually
it's a woman, summer, or any kind of happiness.

Melodrama

La luz del alba daba lucidez al canto de un pájaro en el jardín.
Cantaba como si lo supiera todo clarísimamente.
Yo desperté con miedo
y tú dormías haciendo mohínes, tal vez esperando una piedad.
El pájaro lo entendía todo. Cada signo
le era claro.
Yo descifro las cosas con lentitud y cansancio
y siempre he querido una vida más explícita.
Mi pantalón colgaba de un clavito
y era muy cómodo a la mirada,
colgaba bello y vulgar:
un objeto real, no signo, no cifra en la primera luz.
Nada qué descifrar, sólo un poco de pena evidente
porque caía laxo y abatido como un trapo. Y entonces
en su caída
empezó a dibujarnos, y se hizo signo, y qué feroz.

¿Tú aún sigues esperando en tu sueño una piedad?

Melodrama

The early morning gave a sharpness to the birdsong in the garden.
The bird sang as if it knew it all so clearly.
I woke up in fear
and you slept on making faces, maybe hoping for some mercy.
The bird understood everything. Each sign to it
was clear.
I decipher things slowly and with exhaustion
and always wanted a more clear-cut life.
My pants hung on a nail
and were comfortable to look at,
they hung beautiful and vulgar:
a real object, not a sign, or a figure in first light.
Not much there to decipher, just a shred of sadness
as they dropped slack and dejected like a rag. Then
as they fell
they started drawing us, and made a sign, and how fierce.

Still hoping for some mercy in your sleep?

Este olor, su otro

Mi hermana mayor pica perejil
      con habilidad que se diría congénita,
y el olor viaja instantáneo a fundirse
      con su otro.
Su otro está en una lejana canasta de hierbas de sazón
que bajaba del techo, una canasta
      ahora piedra fósil
suspendida
en el aire de nuestra cocina que se acabó.
El perejil anunciaba a mi padre, Don Harumi,
esperando su sopa frugal.
      Gracias de este país:
un japonés que no perdonaba
¡la ausencia en la mesa de ese secreto local de cocina!
Creo que usted adentraba ese secreto en otro más grande
para componer la belleza de su orden casero
      que ligaba
familia y usos y trucos de esta tierra.
Los hijos de su antiguo alrededor
      hoy somos comensales solos
y diezmados
y comemos la cena del Día de los Difuntos
      esparciendo
perejil en la sopa. Ya la yerba sólo es sazón, aroma
      sin poder.
Nuestras casas, Don Harumi, están caídas.

This Scent, Its Other

My big sister chops parsley
        with a deftness you could say is innate,
and the scent wafts and melts instantly
          with its other.
Its other is in a faraway basket of savory herbs
that once hung down from the roof, a basket
         now a fossil
suspended
in the air of our long-ago kitchen.
Parsley would announce that my father, Don Harumi,
awaited his frugal soup.
            Thanks from this country:
a Japanese man who would never forgive
the local secret's absence at the table!
I think you folded that secret into another one greater
to compose the beauty of your ordered home
          that blended
family and savvy and knacks of this land.
Children of your old environs
        we are lone diners today
divided as tithes
and we eat dinner on Day of the Dead
          scattering
parsley in our soup. The herbs are but seasoning now, aroma
          without power.
Our houses, Don Harumi, are fallen.

Alrededor de mi hermano Juan (i.m.)

Nunca hemos estado tan callados, nunca con las manos así,
quietas y tontas sobre las faldas. Sin embargo, mira:
otras manos nacen de nuestros hombros y se toman, hacen
ruedo
y tú quedas en el centro, pero tendido, desganado, sin jugar.
Ni siquiera muerdes la cristalina fruta del chimbil.
No parece fruta de cactus ni nosotros, sin los aspavientos
de la circunstancia, tus hermanos.
Según costumbre, han colgado una lámpara en la puerta de la calle.
¿Ves en la plaza un ángel
que refulge más que cien lámparas?
Un amigo psiquiatra me ha dicho que es un sueño compensatorio.
Si puedes verlo ahora, dínoslo
con una señal mínima, no rompas tu serenidad
por una noticia que probablemente ya no nos consuele.
La bicicleta que compraste trabajando en el desyerbe
ha venido
y se ha parado en la puerta como un flaco caballo.
Tú dirás que yo arreglo las cosas,
              pero hay una paloma dormida en su montura.
¿Oyes en la habitación contigua
el apurado traqueteo de la máquina de coser?
Es mamá
que entalla su viejo traje negro a su nuevo encorvamiento.
Nuestra antigua batea se ve bastante desubicada
en esta casa de aspirante clase media, pero ahora tú ves
              el cuerpo que allí se baña, el cuerpo de siempre,
incorrupto en agua de eucalipto.
Algún día todos seremos ese cuerpo, los ocho a tu alrededor.
Hoy entra tú en él como en una cripta viva.

Around My Brother Juan (i.m.)

We've never been so quiet, not with our hands like this,
immobile and dumb on our laps. Now look:
more hands rise up between our shoulders and hold one another,
in a ring
with you in the middle, lying there, listless, not playing.
You won't even bite the chimbil's crystal fruit.
It doesn't seem like cactus fruit to us either, not without all the
                                        fussings
of circumstance, your siblings.
Following custom, they've hung a lamp on the streetside door.
See the angel in the plaza
that glows brighter than a hundred lamps?
A psychiatrist friend told me it's a compensatory dream.
If you see it, let us know
with just a tiny sign, but don't disturb your peace
with news that won't comfort us now.
The bicycle you got with what you made weeding
has come
and it waits by the door like a skinny horse.
You're going to say I'm handy with things,
       but there's a dove asleep on its saddle.
Can you hear in the next room
the hurried clatter of the sewing machine?
It's Mom
tailoring her old black dress to her hunchy new back.
Our rickety washtub looks quite out of place
in this striving and middle-class home, but now you see
       the body bathing in it, the always and everyday body,
uncorrupted in eucalyptus water.
We will all be that body someday, we eight around you.
You'll go inside it today like it's a living crypt.

Mamá cumple 75 años

Cinco cuyes han caído
degollados, sacrificados, a tus pies de reina vieja.
Sangre celebra siempre tu cumpleaños, recíbela
en una escudilla
donde pueda cuajar un signo brillante
    además del cuchillo.
La bombilla de luz coincide con tu cabeza dormida
y te aureola: comenzamos a quererte
     con cierta piedad,
pero tus ojos
tus ojos se abren rápidos como avisados, y revive en ellos
un animal de ternura demasiado severa.
Tus ojos de ajadísimo alrededor
son el resto indemne
del personaje central que fuiste entre nosotros,
     cuando alta y enhiesta
alargabas el candil hacia la oscuridad
y llamabas susurrando
a nadie. Las sombras en el muro y los gatos
    detrás de la frontera terrible
eran inocentes. Tú, señora, eras el miedo.

Cinco cuyes pronto estarán servidos en la mesa.
Otros eran los del rito curador, los de entrañas abiertas y sensitivas
que revelaban nuestras enfermedades.
Estos son de diente, de presa. No dirán
que tú eres nuestra más antigua dolencia.

Mama Turns 75

Five cuyes have fallen
slaughtered, sacrificed, at your aged queen's feet.
Blood always celebrates your birthday, receive it
in a bowl
where it can congeal into a brilliant sign
            as it may on the blade.
The light bulb coincides with your sleeping head
and exalts you: we begin loving you
                with certain piety,
but your eyes
your eyes quickly open as if warned, reviving in them
an animal of harsh tenderness.
Your withered eyes of enfolded skin
are the unscathed remainder
of the main character you played among us,
            when upright and tall
you stretched the lamp into the darkness
and called out in whispers
to no one. The shadows on the wall and the cats
            beyond the terrible border
were innocent. You, Señora, were the fear.

Five cuyes will soon be served at the table.
Others were for healing rites, with open and sentient entrails
that revealed our illnesses.
These are for teeth, our prey. They will not say
that you are our oldest malady.

La muriente

Tus hijas pasan llevándote olorosas sopitas
para alimentar tu vaga substancia:
oh, ya eres de agua, de casi nada, de agua
o de lentos movimientos como esculturas de la consunción.
Yo entro a tu cuarto de muriente suavizando mi presencia
                    y mirándote de soslayo:
si te miro de frente siento que soy tu testigo perverso.

Tu antigua y deslumbrante perspicacia aún vive
y sabes que cuando tu cuello se alarga buscando el aire
yo ruego que se alargue hacia el mito:
tú decías que las cabezas se arrancaban de los cuerpos
y volaban
desgreñadas, hambrientas, mordiendo el vano aire.
(Y los regantes decían sí, sí, anoche cruzaron
                    la luz de mi lámpara)
Tengo la carne como en salmuera,
muerde si te salva. Lo dije para que sonrieras.
Tú nunca morderías carne de idiota, no dices.
Lo hubieras dicho con displicente humor
                        y una palabrota.
Bromeo para el tiempo de la pena. Tú sabes cómo es eso:
tu llanto desgarrado por mi padre muerto
fue haciéndose suave y ritual, más homenaje
que llanto.

Frente a ti, ya estamos en ese esfuerzo.

Our Lady of Salt

Your daughters walk by bringing fragrant soups
to nourish the haze of your substance:
oh, you're all made of water, near nothing, just water
or slow movements of wasting sculptures.
I enter your room as I soften my presence
                    looking at you sidelong:
to face you will feel like I'm your evil witness.

Your splintering shrewdness is still quite alive
and you know that when your neck cranes for air
I beg it to stretch out to the myth:
you used to tell us about heads that were torn from their bodies
and soared
disheveled, hungry, biting the air.
(Oh yes, said the water workers, they flew across our lantern light
                    last night)
My flesh feels pickled,
a nice big bite could save you. I said that for a smile.
Why the hell would I bite the flesh of an idiot, is what you don't say.
You'd have said it with splintering humor
                    and some swearing.
I banter through this time of grief. You know what it's like:
your harrowing cries for my dead father
grew softer and ceremonious, more homage
than tears.

Facing you, we are of one accord.

Casa joven de dos muertos

(A mi madre y a mi hermano)

La escalera va del patio a la azotea y en el tercer peldaño
el sol relumbra,
el solcito de los condenados relumbra siempre
                y debidamente.

El tercer peldaño es una estación
donde el cuerpo es leve y blanco como una pastilla
                y el pensamiento intenso. Y todo es tibio
menos los propios huesos.
                Por eso
haya invierno en todo el hemisferio, pero haya siempre el milagro del
                                    sol en la escalera.
Las almitas sentadas allí descansaban como al borde de un abismo
y a veces nos miraban como si nosotros fuéramos el abismo.
Mi casa es joven para tener un frondoso y primaveral limonero.

Del limonero viene ahora el haiku del poeta Moritake:

> *Cae un pétalo de la flor*
> *y de nuevo sube a la rama*
> *Ah, es una mariposa.*

Una equivocación bella y hórrida
                cuando sobrevuelan el patio dos mariposas pálidas.

Young House of Two Deaths

(To my mother and my brother)

The stairs go from the yard to the roof and at the third step
the sun shimmers,
the sunshine of the sentenced always shimmers
        like it should.

The third step is a station
where the body is light and white like a pill
        and intense thought. And everything is warm
except your own bones.
        That's why
though it's winter across the hemisphere, the miracle of sun will
        always be on the stairs.
The little souls rested there like on the edge of an abyss
and sometimes would watch us like we were the abyss.
My house is young for a lush spring lemon tree.

From the lemon tree now comes Moritake's haiku:

> *A flower petal falls*
> *and floats back to the branch.*
> *Ah, a butterfly.*

A lovely and horrid equivocation
        when two pale butterflies hover over the courtyard.

Interior de hospital

Cómo envidiamos el largo cuello
de las garzas que se posan en la cumbrera.
Ellas pueden doblar el cuello y dormir sobre la música
        de sus corazones.
Nuestros latidos están en la línea verde del monitor cardiaco
                y son el ansia que miramos.

Las garzas pueden alzar el cuello como periscopios
cuando sienten el paso de otro nivel de aire. Y ya verán
si lo viajan o lo dejan seguir al Báltico helado.
¡Ah, si nosotros, pájaros de camisón blanco,
pudiéramos estirar el cuello
por encima de esta lenta y dolorosa danza…!
Aquí la realidad se presenta como un sutil cambio de niveles,
pero me falta atrevimiento
para asomar mi cabeza a un conocimiento definitivo:
                sólo ignoro y respiro.
A veces siento el paso de una realidad primera y prodigiosa
                y me encojo
para que no se lleve mi cabeza, o la seccione.

En Berlín una cabeza volando es cosa indiferente.
En mi pueblo es un mito peligroso.

Hospital Interior

How we envy the long neck
of the herons up on the roof ridge.
They can fold their necks and sleep upon
                        the music of their hearts.
Our heartbeats are on the cardiac monitor's green line
                        and we watch their yearnings.

The herons lift their necks like periscopes
when they sense a new layer of air. And then we see
if they surf it or let it go toward the freezing Baltic.
Ah, if we, white-gowned birds,
could only stretch our necks
over this slow and painful dance . . . !
Here reality shows up like a subtle shift in levels,
but I don't have the nerve
to stick my neck into definitive knowledge:
                        I breathe unaware.
Sometimes I feel the passing of a prime and prodigious reality
                        and I cringe
so it won't take my head, or cut it off.

A flying head in Berlin is a matter of indifference.
Back at home it's a dangerous myth.

La tejedora

Mirando
a la muchacha que teje en telar de cintura
me aprieto
solitario y concupiscente
contra la yerba que crece en esta colina de mi pereza.
Mi oído
cree escuchar
el chirrido de la tierra girando sobre su eje.
Si en alguna parte suena, sería aquí.
Y entonces recuerdo el globo terráqueo de escritorio
donde jugaba
a buscar un lugar para vivir, apuntándolo con el dedo,
al azar.

Tu teoría, Copérnico,
explica la alternancia del día y la noche,
mientras los hombres buscamos
en la tierra
un lugar para vivir.

La tejedora
intercala la lanzadera
entre las mil hebras del telar, y ya se puede ver
las figuras que idealiza:
un colibrí
frente a la flor del floripondio.

Su mano
cogiendo la lanzadera que parece puñal
insinúa
otro movimiento, el que puede herir,
pero no
este es un lugar apacible
y todo se mueve con bondad.

The Weaver

Watching
the young woman weave on the backstrap loom
I press
fervid and alone
against my grassy hill of sloth.
My ear
thinks it hears
the screech of the earth on its axis.
If you can hear it somewhere, it's got to be here.
And I remember the globe on the desk
where I played
at looking for a place to live, stopping it with my finger,
                    at random.

Your theory, Copernicus,
explains night and day's alternations
while the rest of us
comb the earth
for someplace to live.

                The weaver
rocks the shuttle
through thousands of threads, and behold
her idealized figures:
a hummingbird
at the angel's trumpet blossom.

Grabbing
the dagger-like shuttle
                her hand hints
at another move, one that could hurt,
                    but no
this place is peaceable
        and everything here moves kindly along.

¿Sería posible, Copérnico,
sumar los movimientos de su mano
con los infinitos otros de la misma índole
y hacer uno solo
para que la vida que gira sobre tu teoría
sea rápidamente bella
como en este tejido de Cajamarca?

Is it possible, Copernicus,
to sum the movements of her hand
with its infinite others
and make one
so the life that gyrates around your theory
brings a swift splendor
like on this weaving from Cajamarca?

MUSEO INTERIOR | INNER MUSEUM

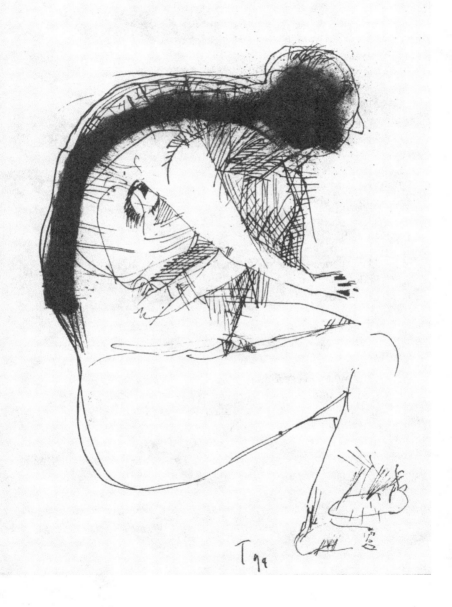

La gallina ciega (Goya)

Mueves el pie en el gozne del tobillo
        como llevan la música los tímidos, y luego
llamado
entras a jugar sin mucha intención a la gallina ciega.
Y así errático, así torpe
oyes las voces de los corrillos, imaginas
la cadencia plúmbea de los potitos en pera.
Las voces son muy verbales, pero entre ellas debes recoger una
que te releve.
Esta casa no es tu demagógica y polvorienta plazuela
donde rápidamente cambiabas tu rol
con otro chiquillo humilde
        que no ha venido.
Estas que oyes son tus nuevas voces. Pudieron ser
para tu previsible resentimiento, pero no.
El agnóstico que te confía su deseo de creer en Dios,
la descasada que parece vulnerable como chivita en pampa,
el ortodoxo y el que reconsidera las cosas, todos
son honestos
a su manera.
No son para tu resentimiento, pero tampoco para tu entusiasmo.

Continúa con ese ánimo. Así
siempre podrás, como otras veces, dejar la ronda,
siempre podrás hacerles con los dedos una figura obscena
        y largarte.

Blind Man's Bluff (Goya)

Your foot gently bobs from the crook of your ankle
        like shyness to music, and
you're it
it's your turn now to play Blind Man's Bluff.
So awkward, you bungle
to the coterie's voices, imagining
the soft leaden plunge of those baby-jar melons.
The voices will prattle, so pick one among them
to relieve you.
This house isn't your dusty demagogic town square
where you'd be sure to trade places
with some other poor kid
          who's not here.
What you hear are fresh voices. They could very well stoke
your predictable rancor, but no.
The agnostic who confesses his desire to know God,
the vixen unwed like a naked young goat,
the orthodox and she who reconsiders things, all
are honest
in their way.
They're not for your resentment, or for your zeal.

Keep up with those spirits. That's how
you shall, as you always, abandon the round,
give them the finger with both obscene hands
             and get away.

Los paralizados (George Segal)

Un inexplicable y silencioso pavor
nos detiene de repente en las calles, quedamos
paralizados, detenidos
                    en lo que estábamos,
como los animalitos aprisionados en un transparente pisapapeles de
                                                    acrílico.

Nadie luce pose preparada,
nadie tiene dignidad de estatua.
Algunos estamos congelados ante el escaparate de una tienda de
                                                juegos de mesa
mirando infinitamente un ajedrez de piedra huamanga.
Sobre el tablero sólo han dispuesto siete piezas
y un cartelito reta al clavado público:
                    "Jaque mate en dos jugadas."
Yo no tengo la respuesta. Me ocupa el esfuerzo
de mantener la memoria en un punto verdadero y entrañable
para volver.

La inmovilidad de las piezas del ajedrez no es la nuestra.
A ellas las engrandece un combate, sus próximos
                    dos movimientos
finales y fatales
que matarán un rey.
Nosotros despertaremos de este detenimiento
para concluir nuestra acción interrumpida, la que iba
a continuarse con otra
                    igual de enésima y gregaria.

The Paralyzed (George Segal)

An inexplicable noiseless dread
stops us dead in our tracks, we're left
paralyzed, confined
to what we were,
like tiny animals imprisoned in a clear acrylic paperweight.

No one looks at all prepared,
no one has a statue's dignity.
Some of us are frozen at a board-game shop window
staring infinitely into a Huamanga-stone chess set.
Only seven pieces on the board
and a little card prodding the dumbfounded audience:
"Checkmate in two moves."
I have no answer. I'm engrossed in what it takes
to save my memory at a real and winning point
and make it back.

The inertness of chessmen is not our affair.
They're magnified by combat, the next
final and fatal
two moves
that will kill a king.
We will wake up from this scrutiny
to finish what we were doing, that which was
about to carry on with the other
of the nth herdish degree.

El grito (Edvard Munch)

Bajo el puente de Chosica el río se embalsa
y es de sangre,
        pero la sangre no me es creída.
Los poetas hablan en lengua figurada, dicen.
Y yo porfío: no es el reflejo del cielo crepuscular, bermejo,
        en el agua que hace de espejo.

¿Oyen el grito de la mujer
que contempla el río desde la baranda
        pensando en las alegorías de Heráclito y Manrique
y que de pronto vio la sangre al natural fluyendo?
Ella es mujer verdadera. Por su flacura
        no la sospechen metafísica.
Su flacura se debe a la fisiología de su grito:
Recoge sus carnes en su boca
        y en el grito
          las consume.
El viento del atardecer quiere arrancarle la cabeza,
miren cómo la defiende, cómo la sujeta
        con sus manos
          a sus hombros: un gesto
finalmente optimista en su desesperación.
Viene gritando, gritando, desbordada gritando.
Ella no está restringida a la lengua figurada:
        hay matarifes
y no cielos bermejos, grita.
Yo escribo y mi estilo es mi represión. En el horror
sólo me permito este poema silencioso.

The Scream (Edvard Munch)

The river dams under the Chosica Bridge
and it's with blood,
        but I have no faith in the blood's conceit.
Poets speak in figurative language, they say.
And I persist: that's no reflection of a crepuscular, auburn sky,
        in the mirrored waters flowing by.

Can they hear the scream of the woman
who stares at the river from the railing
        thinking in allegories of Heraclitus and Manrique
and who suddenly saw that rush of raw blood?
She is a real woman. Her skin and bones
        parry suspicions of metaphysics.
Her gauntness is due to her scream's physiology:
She gathers her flesh in her mouth
        and consumes it
        in her scream.
The dusky winds try to rip off her head,
watch her defend it, how she fastens it
        to her shoulders
        with her hands: optimistic
at last in her late desperation.
Screaming, screaming, gushing with screams.
Untethered by figurative language:
        there are slaughtermen
she screams, not auburn skies.
I write and my style is my repression. Amid the horror
I allow myself this quiet poem.

CODA

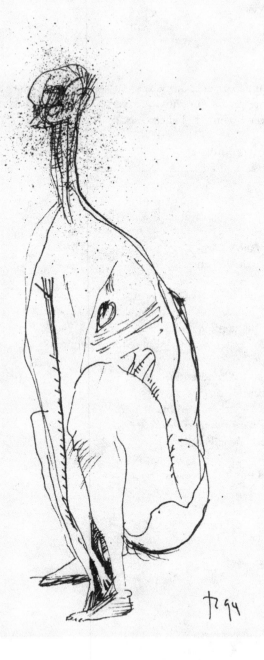

De la poesía

El niño entró en la sombra de su árbol de extramuros
donde dejaba diariamente sus quehaceres de intestino.
Y si otro niño en árbol vecino se acuclillaba
                y se aliviaba
        brotaba entre ambos
la honrosa complicidad en la depuración
                del buen animal.
Esta vez, sin embargo,
una visión suspende al niño, lo fija
con estupor
        bajo su árbol:
en medio de una anterior limpieza
                crecía
una incipiente y trémula plantita.
        Y lo estremeció la imaginación del viaje
de la pequeña menestra
a lo largo de su cuerpo, su recorrido indemne,
incontaminado
        y defendiendo
en su íntimo y delicado centro
                el embrión vivo.
Y en la memoria del niño,
        con difícil contento,
comenzó a elevarse para siempre
la planta mínima, tu principio, tu verde banderita,
                poesía.

On Poetry

The boy stepped into the shade of his tree outside the city
where each day he left behind his intestinal chores.
And if a boy at a neighboring tree squatted down
        to relieve himself
     between them would sprout
the noble complicity in the purging
        of fine animals.
This time, however,
a vision suspends the boy, with wonder
he stares
      beneath his tree:
from the middle of a previous cleanse
        there grew
an early and quivering seedling.
     And he shivered imagining the journey
of the beany bit of stew
down the whole length of his body, its path unscathed,
unspoiled
      and defending
in his private and delicate insides
        the live embryo.
And in the boy's memory,
     with difficult joy,
it began to rise forever
that tiny plant, your commencement, your baby flag so green,
        poetry.

Arte poética

Deja tu alfiler de entomólogo, poeta:
las palabras no son mariposas con teta.

Sentado en la cima del osario
preguntas: ¿seré yo el nuevo notario?

Pasan muchas frases de hombro caído,
tú las quieres con un poquito de sonido.

Las palabras, o mejor, las vampiro
ya vienen volando con lujurioso suspiro.

Pronto serás tú, entre gozoso y aterrado,
el mamado.

Ars Poetica

Poet, put down the entomologist's pin:
words aren't butterflies' tits you can win.

Seated on top of that charnel of bones
you ask: will I be the new scrivener enthroned?

Clauses come forth from your shoulders hunched down,
you want to grace them with inklings of sound.

Words, as it were, those damned vamps on the prowl
hover and plunge with lascivious howls.

Soon it will be you, your ecstatic knees buckling,
                    a suckling.

TRANSLATOR'S ACKNOWLEDGMENTS

It is impossible to quantify the friends, colleagues, mentors, and strangers who have encouraged me to answer the call of this project. With love and debt I thank: Michaela Chirif, whose love of *Historia natural* gave me a place to begin and sowed the idea that maybe it could be translated as a single volume someday, como tal; Eduardo Tokeshi, who set aside hours to talk with me at a hotel cafe in Los Angeles, while it dawned on me that this was a work by not one man, but two; Maya Watanabe, who challenges me and made these translations better; the Watanabe family, for blessings; Gerald Maa and Lawrence-Minh Bùi Davis, for discovery and belief; Julia Wong Kcomt, for semiotic rigor; Anna Kazumi Stahl, whose grace had forged a way; and the early and bright-eyed giant, Jennifer Shuye.

Were this book mine, it would be dedicated to my causitas Garren and Dae Han Imani Chew, and to Héctor Velásquez, José Carlos Baron Copello, David Lloyd, Gabriel Alejandro Giorgi, Seth Michelson, Carlos Yushimito del Valle, Naoki Sakai, Akira Mizuta Lippit, Viet Thanh Nguyen, Jacob Israel Littleton, and Anika Leila Davoll Gibbons. I thank William Rowe, Brandon Som, Emmanuel Alberto Velayos, Rick Snyder, Brian Shimoda, Jordan A. Yamaji Smith, Michelle Clayton, Eleanor Steele Billington, Mohamed Sheriff, Umair Kazi, Julia Sanches, Clara Chu, Karen Tei Yamashita, Imani e. Wilson, Elaine Hiyoung Kim, Luna Yasui, Isabela Seong Leong Quintana, Nigel de Juan Hatton, Tessa Liebman, Rebecca Rutkoff, Mayumo Inoue, Edgar A. M. Fraire, Lindsay Rebecca Nelson-Santos, Ana Paulina Lee, Nada Ayad, Ayana McNair, Yukari Yanagino, Julián Liu, Cedric Howshan Bien-Gund, Robi Roman, Michael Cucher, Aditi Das, Beth Staples, Elaine Yee, Jeehyun Lim, Shayna Kessel, Soraya Sélène, Sabeena Setia, India Ornelas, Donald Pease, Donatella Izzo, Cindy I-Fen Cheng, Ignacio López-Calvo, Ricardo A. Wilson II, Anna Koós, Eva Buchmiller, Sylvia Kwon, Mia Warren, Donna Loghmanee Feldman, Efraín Kristal, Roberto Ignacio Díaz, Anuradha Needham, Steve Volk, Galus Halasz, Cecillia

Chu, Pashmina Murthy, Rasmia Kirmani, Jeanhee Kim, Hala Halim, Feng-Mei Heberer, Rebecca R. Tsurumi, Chandler Chang, Rosie Moreno, Aidé Perez Soto, David Soto, the achistas at Bread Loaf, Fred Moten, all my language teachers, and my parents.

Love and prosperity to the translation lovers and translation-advocating souls at the National Endowment for the Arts, the Authors Guild, the American Literary Translators Association, and the BIPOC Literary Translators Caucus. Thank you Lisa Bayer, Beth Snead, Elizabeth Adams, Jon Davies, Sarah Jordan, and all the patient folks at the University of Georgia Press and the *Georgia Review*. To those who can decipher my weird conversational Spanish, who overlook my misreadings (current, imminent, strategic, or misguided), and whom I've abused or forgotten: I appreciate you.

Formal opportunities for research and language work over the years have helped improve my Spanish proficiency so that I could engage with others' knowledges about Watanabe and el Perú. These include an NEA Translation Fellowship, graduate support from USC, UCLA, and their respective Deparments of Comparative Literature; and an Oberlin College Alumni Grant. I thank La Pontificia Universidad Católica del Perú for letting me use the library years ago to read student theses on Watanabe; and the Huntington Library, for the resources that it provides to its independent scholars, and for its cool and quiet spaces. Several translations in *Natural History* first appeared in the *Asian American Literary Review*, *Shenandoah*, and on the Japanese American National Museum's *Discover Nikkei* website, which for some time has warmly hosted a variety of things Watanabe. This book has also been made possible by the Smithsonian Asian Pacific American Center.

GEORGIA REVIEW BOOKS